P9-EMM-913

21st Century Skills Library

Century

Skills Library

GLOBAL PERSPECTIVES

EDUCATION

Jason Loeb

South Huntington Pub. Lib.
145 Pidgeon Hill Rd.
Huntington Sta., N.Y. 11746

Cherry Lake Publishing
Ann Arbor, Michigan

Published in the United States of America by Cherry Lake Publishing
Ann Arbor, Michigan
www.cherrylakepublishing.com

Content Adviser: Ward W. Weldon, PhD, Associate Professor of Policy Studies, College
of Education, University of Illinois at Chicago

Photo Credits: Cover and page 1, © WizData, Inc., used under license from Shutterstock,
Inc.; pages 4 and 22, © Robert Harding Picture Library Ltd/Alamy; page 7, © Hemis/
Alamy; page 9, © The Print Collector/Alamy; page 10, © North Wind Picture Archives/
Alamy; page 12, © vario images GmbH & Co.KG/Alamy; page 14, © Digital Archive
Japan/Alamy; page 15, © Jim West/Alamy; page 16, © Kirk Treakle/Alamy; page 19, ©
Andrew Fox/Alamy; page 20, © John Birdsall/Alamy; page 25, © Kees Metselaar/Alamy;
page 27, © Lisa F. Young, used under license from Shutterstock, Inc.

Map by XNR Productions Inc.

Copyright ©2008 by Cherry Lake Publishing
All rights reserved. No part of this book may be reproduced or utilized in any form or by any
means without written permission from the publisher.

Library of Congress Cataloging-in-Publication Data
Loeb, Jason, 1983–
 Education / By Jason Loeb.
   p. cm.—(Global perspectives)
 Includes index.
 ISBN-13: 978-1-60279-124-4
 ISBN-10: 1-60279-124-4
 1. Education—Juvenile literature. I. Title. II. Series.
 LB1556.L64 2008
 370.9—dc22   2007040102

---

*Cherry Lake Publishing would like to acknowledge the work of
The Partnership for 21st Century Skills.
Please visit* www.21stcenturyskills.org *for more information.*

TABLE OF CONTENTS

CHAPTER ONE

EDUCATION AS A GLOBAL ISSUE

*Students in a Japanese elementary school work on a
lesson. Many schools in Japan are crowded.*

Johnny Tuttle sat in the lobby of the conference center, grinning as he
looked down at the letter he had received the day before. After all of the
applications, essays, and interviews, he had finally gotten accepted into
the school he wanted. Just then, Marie Pepin, a student from Canada, and

Kazutaka Ito, a student from Japan, approached him, curious to see what he was so happy about.

"Hey, Johnny! What's going on?" asked Marie.

Johnny proudly replied, "I'm just admiring my acceptance letter to this awesome **magnet school** back home. I'm so excited!"

"That's great!" said Marie. "You're lucky to have the opportunity to go to a school where you can get a great education. Most kids in the world today don't have that kind of opportunity."

Kazutaka offered his congratulations also. "That's wonderful news, Johnny! How many students are enrolled in the school?"

"About 500. It's pretty selective," Johnny replied.

"Wow!" exclaimed Kazutaka, amazed by the figure. "That's small compared to my school. It has 1,000 students, and our classrooms are always overcrowded."

"Why can't they just move students to other schools, so that your building isn't so full?" asked Marie.

"It's not that simple," explained Kazutaka. "Some schools are better than others and are harder to get into. Because of standardized testing and **tracking**, some students can only go to certain schools. Some schools are too far away from home to commute. And many schools are already overcrowded."

21st Century Content

In the 21st century, every country is connected. Whether it is through the economy, communications, or politics, one country can be affected by events in countries halfway around the world. This is often referred to as globalization.

Globalization has had a big impact on schools in the United States, Canada, and many other countries. For instance, the U.S. population is more diverse now than ever. New immigrants from all over the world make their way to the United States for greater opportunities. This affects the student population in many schools. Today, it is common to see Asian and Hispanic students sitting next to African American and white students whose families have been in the country for generations.

What other changes brought about by globalization have affected schools where you live?

"Kaz, what makes one school better than another?" asked Johnny.

Before he could respond, Marie—who was now thinking about all schools—had even more questions. "Who pays for education? Who has the right to an education?" she asked.

"Isn't that why we're here?" replied Kazutaka, with a smile.

Johnny, Marie, and Kazutaka were part of a group of students from around the world at the International Global Issues, Global Solutions Summit in Calgary, Canada. They were there to discuss issues facing leaders around the world.

CHAPTER TWO

MORE THAN JUST TEXTBOOKS, TEACHERS, AND HOMEWORK

Students in a school in Senegal listen as their teacher explains something to a classmate.

The crowd of students sat down in the conference room for a discussion. Ronia, a student from Israel, rose out of her chair to pose a question to the summit.

"What exactly does it mean to have a *good* education?" she asked.

"To answer that, Ronia, we have to look at the history of education," explained Idrissa Diouf, a student from the West African nation of Senegal.

"We should look at what the primary goals for education are. Only then can we define what a good education is, where we may be coming up short, and what solutions we can come up with."

Despite the differences between school systems in different countries, they all share one primary function: to teach children to read and write. Yet education is more than just textbooks, teachers, and homework. Education carries an important mission. The word *education* comes from the Latin words *educare*, meaning "to nourish" or "to bring up" and *educere*, meaning "to impress a pattern." Education is about preparing students to become knowledgeable and active citizens of the world.

An educated person should be trained in a variety of subjects, including reading, writing, math, and science. Most students don't excel in every area, but a good education strengthens each student's knowledge of required subjects. It ensures that students develop at least basic **proficiency** in each subject.

Education can be traced back as far as human history. The earliest humans had to learn how to survive by finding ways to hunt and cook their food. They had to make their own clothing and find shelter. They had to teach these survival skills to their young, so that they would survive, too. Education involves both learning and teaching.

Most people say that **formal education** began in ancient Greece with the Greek philosophers. Scholars from far and wide would come to listen to and learn from great thinkers such as Socrates, Plato, and Aristotle. Greek mythology and fables were used to teach children valuable life lessons.

As time marched on, trading routes were formed, empires

Socrates was an ancient Greek philosopher who taught by asking a series of questions that would lead his students to an answer.

expanded, and human thought and culture spread. Western European countries such as Great Britain, France, and Italy became the cultural centers of Europe. Western cultural influences, such as music, art, science, and literature, eventually spread to the Far East. Places like India and China were centers of spiritual growth. Saudi Arabia, Israel, and Iraq became religious centers.

*Spanish missionaries established many missions in the Americas
and taught the Native Americans their European culture.*

European culture and knowledge eventually crossed the Atlantic Ocean
to the Americas. British and French colonists spread their literature,
art, and language throughout North America. Spanish conquistadors
colonized and expanded into South America. Despite the early conflicts
that arose between the colonists and the Native Americans, there was much
that the two sides learned from one another. Native Americans taught the
explorers and colonists important hunting and survival techniques. The
newcomers introduced the Native Americans to horses and guns. Christian

missionaries taught Native Americans new languages, new forms of art, and new customs.

Over time, education became more formal. Schools and universities were established in almost every country. School systems adopted their own unique approaches to teaching and learning. While educational practices vary from country to country, one thing remains the same—education is about spreading knowledge and culture to a country's citizens. It is an important way for people to express and share ideas and knowledge with one another.

◆ ◆ ◆

"So you see, Ronia," continued Idrissa, "education has been around for a long time, and almost everyone agrees that a good education means sharing knowledge and culture."

"I get it!" exclaimed Ronia. "But we should keep in mind that while we know what a good education means, and why it is important, there are different ways of educating people. Not everyone learns the same way."

Missionaries travel to other countries with the goal of spreading their faith. They often establish schools that teach religion along with other subjects. Early missionaries in America believed that their European languages and culture were superior to those of the Native Americans. They believed that they were helping the Native Americans become more civilized by teaching them their religious beliefs, languages, and customs. But Native Americans often resisted learning the ways of the missionaries. They struggled to hold on to their own religious beliefs and cultures.

Do you think that missionaries should try to teach their religions, languages, and customs to people in other countries? Why or why not?

CHAPTER THREE

WHAT IS THE BEST WAY TO EDUCATE?

Children sit on a dirt floor at a school in Mozambique. In many places, schools lack basic supplies and furniture.

Kazutaka listened closely to the discussion and rose to speak.

"One question that troubles me is why some countries are farther behind academically than other countries," he said. "If leaders in each country understand the value of a good education, then why are there kids in some countries who don't have good schools to go to?"

Marie stood up to try and respond. "Maybe we should discuss the way a few countries have structured their school systems," she said. "Maybe we can try and figure out why some have been more successful than others."

In many Asian countries, such as Japan, students excel academically. This is because of their high standards and the high level of competition. Japan has a **compulsory** education system. All students must attend at least six years of elementary school, three years of junior high school, and three years of senior high. Because Japan is densely populated, there is a lot of competition to get into the best schools. Most high schools, colleges and universities, and even a few middle and elementary schools require entrance exams and essays to determine which students will be accepted.

Many schools in Japan are specialty schools. Some specialize in mathematics and science, and some in the arts. Most students in these schools take classes that will help them get into college. Their "track," or the level of difficulty of the classes they will take, is based on their **standardized test** scores. The Japanese school system has helped the country's students become some of the most consistent academic achievers in the world.

Because of standardized testing and the fierce competition to get into the best schools, many Japanese students attend special preparation

Some schools in Japan specialize in a particular subject, such as science.

schools outside of their regular classes. These special schools are called *juku*. They are aimed at preparing students for the very difficult entrance exams that they will need to take to get into the schools they want to attend.

The Ministry of Education, Culture, Sports, Science and Technology (MEXT) manages Japan's school system. MEXT helps fund the schools' resources and establishes educational programs. MEXT decides what will be taught in the schools and even what textbooks the students will learn from.

Even though most Japanese students do well in school, some Japanese are critical of their education system. They think that MEXT has too much control over the school system.

Students in Michigan take a standardized test.

Another criticism is that standardized testing is too stressful. Many people argue that Japanese schools tend to put too much value on good test scores. They say that good test scores do not always mean that students

Some people in Japan think that their schools are too structured.

are actually learning. Another complaint is that their schools do not offer enough individualized attention. Some Japanese people believe that the schools are too structured, allowing no flexibility or creativity. Others find the tracking system too limiting. They complain that it does not offer a **comprehensive education**.

Schools in the United States offer a more comprehensive education. This means that schools teach every subject, including math, science, art, language, and history. Most American students attend school through high school, but in some states students can drop out of school at age 16 if they want to. The majority of students attend free public schools in their area. Some students pay tuition to attend private schools. Most public and private schools are divided into three levels: elementary school, junior high school (or middle school), and senior high school.

Public education in the United States is funded on three different levels. The first level of funding comes from the local or city school district. The district provides money and funds for the schools in that district to run adequately. The second level of funding comes from the state government. The state can decide what is to be taught and what

21st Century Content

The literacy rate of a country is an official statistic that measures what percentage of its people over the age of 15 can read and write at a basic level. Here are some sample literacy rates:

Country	Literacy Rate
United States	99%
Japan	99%
Canada	99%
Israel	97.1%
United Arab Emirates	77.9%
Nepal	48.6%
Senegal	39.3%

Why do you think the literacy rate is different from one country to the next? What factors do you think contribute to how high or low a country's literacy rate is?
(Source: *Central Intelligence Agency—The World Factbook 2007*)

Learning & Innovation Skills

Religion in schools is a hot topic in education. In some countries, such as Egypt and the Netherlands, the government provides funds for both religious and nonreligious schools. In Cuba, the government forbids religious schools. In the United States, the Constitution prevents the government from funding religious schools. This is because the Constitution requires the separation of church and state. Religious institutions and government institutions must be separate in all matters of the law. Religious schools in the United States and many other places around the world are private. The money to run these schools comes from the people who attend. These schools are allowed to teach religion without the government interfering.

What is your opinion about religion in schools? Should it be taught? Should the government provide funds for schools that include it in their curriculums?

educational standards the schools should follow. The state can also give state and local standardized tests to the students, in order to make sure that they are improving according to the state standards. These tests may be different from state to state. The third level of funding comes from the federal government. The U.S. government has an budget of $67.2 billion for education. This money comes from the **taxes** that citizens pay. The government uses the tax money to establish national programs to make sure that schools run properly. Leaders want the country's students to be able to compete with students around the world.

While the United States has a **literacy rate** of 99 percent (see sidebar on page 17), its students frequently score lower in science and mathematics than students in other countries, such as Japan. One federal law that has been passed to help U.S.

Students at an Islamic school in the United Kingdom read the Koran.

students perform better academically is the No Child Left Behind Act of 2001 (NCLB). This act calls for the improvement of students' math and reading skills. It increased the standards for reading and mathematics and measures student improvement each year through standardized testing. These tests show the government if a school's students are meeting required standards, if they have improved and are closer to meeting standards, or if they are not meeting standards at all.

Students listen to their teacher in a school in Cuba. In Cuba,
the government pays to educate all citizens through college.

Some people feel that NCLB is a great way to get students to perform better in school. There have been big improvements in test scores in some schools. People also like the idea that **accountability** for students' progress is placed on teachers and schools. But some people believe that NCLB does not work. Like many Japanese, some people in the United States do not want to focus on testing. They think it is too stressful for students. People also complain that the law gives the U.S. government too much control over the way the states' districts run their schools and what is taught. People argue that the government should not have the right to reward some schools for performing well and punish others for their students' lack of achievement.

Not all education systems are like those in the United States and Japan. For example, in many Middle Eastern countries—such as Afghanistan, Egypt, and the United Arab Emirates—religion is taught as a subject in school.

In some countries, women are not encouraged to attend school. In Afghanistan, for example, when the Taliban government was in power, women were not allowed to attend school. When the Taliban was overthrown, women were once again allowed to go to school.

In some countries, the government fully funds education. In Cuba, for example, because it is a communist country, the government pays for everyone's education all the way through college.

◆ ◆ ◆

"So each country has its own way of educating its people. Does this mean that there is no right way or wrong way?" asked Kazutaka.

"That's right, Kaz," Ronia answered. "There is no right or wrong way to educate people in your country. All you can do is provide the best education you can with the resources you have."

CHAPTER FOUR

WHAT'S AT STAKE?

Boys harvest grain in Ethiopia. In many developing countries, children have to work to help their families survive.

Johnny mustered up the courage to raise his hand.

"I have one thing that has been on my mind the whole day," said Johnny, a little timidly. "I realized today that I am lucky to have such a great education. But what about the students who aren't as lucky? What happens to kids if their countries or their families cannot provide a good education for them?"

The other students thought about Johnny's question. They began discussing what is at stake for those who are not lucky enough to have a good education. They knew that some countries such as the United States, Canada, and Japan provide a good education for most students. But what about **developing countries**, those in which leaders struggle to provide people with basic needs?

Most kids in **developed countries** can get a good education. There are students in other countries, however, who are not as lucky. Developing countries, such as Senegal and Afghanistan, lack the resources needed for teaching and learning. Many schools don't have basic supplies such as up-to-date textbooks. Things that many students in developed countries take for granted, such as computers, are rare in the classrooms of developing countries.

In countries where poverty is high, many kids have to work to help their families stay alive. This keeps them out of school. Even when kids can get to the classroom, there is often little that is learned. Many come to class weak, tired, and starving, which makes it nearly impossible for them to pay attention.

Learning & Innovation Skills

Many families in Senegal lack proper housing and nutrition. Boys and girls are forced to work to help their families, or they wander the streets looking for food. School is not part of life for these children. Survival is their main concern. Leaders of organizations such as the United Nations Children's Fund (UNICEF) and Education Africa know that education can help lift people out of poverty. Better education brings better income to many families. With the help of UNICEF and Education Africa, Senegal is slowly rebuilding its education system to help provide its children a chance for a better future.

What do you think you can do to be a leader in the fight to provide a brighter future for kids living in poverty—not only around the world but in your own town?

Unfortunately, these are hard issues to overcome. People with limited access to education are unable to get good jobs that would help them break the cycle of poverty. Many world leaders continue to fight for better schools, more funding, and a better future for their children.

"So kids who have limited resources in school and at home have no choice but to live in poverty until things change?" Johnny asked angrily.

"Unfortunately, that has been the case for many years, Johnny," explained Idrissa. "But with more funding, more resources, and more help from other nations, these countries may be able to find some stability. And maybe then, these kids can start going back to school. But the fight has to continue with us."

CHAPTER FIVE

EDUCATING OURSELVES: HOW CAN WE HELP?

UNICEF helped get Indonesian students back into classrooms after tsunamis destroyed many buildings in 2004.

As Johnny, Marie, and Kazutaka left the conference hall, Johnny asked, "How can we help?"

"There are many organizations that are reaching out to countries in need. Maybe we can contact them to see how we can get involved," suggested Kaz.

Education Africa is an organization based in Johannesburg, South Africa. Its main goal is to improve the quality of life in Africa through better education. Support for the organization comes from many countries, including the United States, the United Kingdom, and Austria. To find out more about Education Africa, you can visit its Web site at www.educationafrica.org.

Why do you think leaders in countries such as the United States and Austria are interested in helping developing countries in Africa provide a good education for their people? Hint: Think global.

"Right!" agreed Marie. "But we also need to do some work. We should try to understand the issues by keeping up with the news and reading about education in other countries."

"Maybe we could contact our leaders and representatives, and tell them that this is important. We should all be doing our part to help the cause," added Johnny.

◆ ◆ ◆

A good education is not an easy formula. It requires well-trained teachers, supportive families, willing students, and enough funding to make it happen. Without these things, schools and universities won't produce results. And when an education system doesn't work, it can't help provide solutions to problems like poverty.

◆ ◆ ◆

"In the meantime," concluded Johnny, "we need to appreciate how lucky we are to have access to a good education."

A good education is the foundation for success.

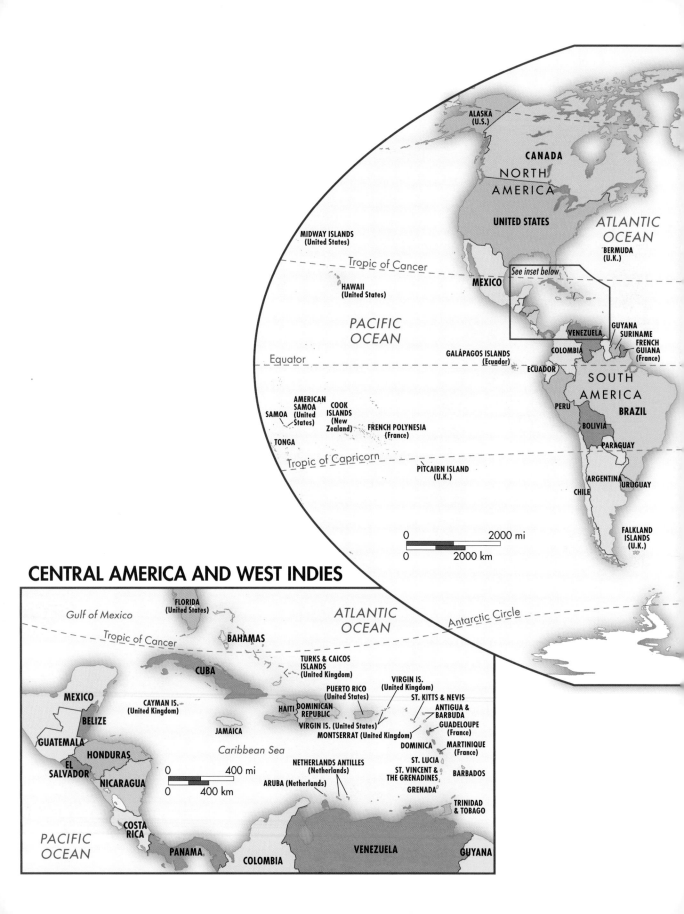

ALASKA
(U.S.)

CANADA

NORTH
AMERICA

UNITED STATES

ATLANTIC
OCEAN

BERMUDA
(U.K.)

MIDWAY ISLANDS
(United States)

Tropic of Cancer

See inset below

MEXICO

HAWAII
(United States)

PACIFIC
OCEAN

GALÁPAGOS ISLANDS
(Ecuador)

VENEZUELA

GUYANA
SURINAME
FRENCH
GUIANA
(France)

COLOMBIA

Equator

ECUADOR

SOUTH
AMERICA

PERU

BRAZIL

AMERICAN
SAMOA
(United
States)

SAMOA

COOK
ISLANDS
(New
Zealand)

FRENCH POLYNESIA
(France)

BOLIVIA

TONGA

PARAGUAY

Tropic of Capricorn

PITCAIRN ISLAND
(U.K.)

ARGENTINA

URUGUAY

CHILE

0   2000 mi

0   2000 km

FALKLAND
ISLANDS
(U.K.)

Antarctic Circle

CENTRAL AMERICA AND WEST INDIES

FLORIDA
(United States)

Gulf of Mexico

ATLANTIC
OCEAN

Tropic of Cancer

BAHAMAS

CUBA

TURKS & CAICOS
ISLANDS
(United Kingdom)

VIRGIN IS.
(United Kingdom)

MEXICO

CAYMAN IS.
(United Kingdom)

PUERTO RICO
(United States)

ST. KITTS & NEVIS

BELIZE

HAITI

DOMINICAN
REPUBLIC

ANTIGUA &
BARBUDA

GUATEMALA

JAMAICA

VIRGIN IS. (United States)

GUADELOUPE
(France)

HONDURAS

Caribbean Sea

MONTSERRAT (United Kingdom)

DOMINICA

MARTINIQUE
(France)

EL
SALVADOR

0   400 mi

NETHERLANDS ANTILLES
(Netherlands)

ST. LUCIA

NICARAGUA

0   400 km

ST. VINCENT &
THE GRENADINES

BARBADOS

ARUBA (Netherlands)

GRENADA

TRINIDAD
& TOBAGO

PACIFIC
OCEAN

COSTA
RICA

PANAMA

COLOMBIA

VENEZUELA

GUYANA

GLOSSARY

accountability (uh-kount-uh-BILL-uh-tee) holding a teacher, student, or school responsible for student achievement

communist (KOM-yuh-nist) describing a way of organizing a country so that all the land, houses, factories, etc., belong to the government or community, and the profits are shared by all

comprehensive education (kom-pri-HEN-siv ej-uh-KAY-shuhn) an education that teaches most, if not all, subjects

compulsory (kuhm-PUHL-suh-ree) required by law

developed countries (dih-VEL-uhpt KUHN-treez) countries with advanced levels of industrialization and generally high incomes; usually the world's richest nations

developing countries (di-VEL-uhp-eeng KUHN-treez) nations in which most people are poor and there is not much industry

diverse (dye-VURSS) varied or assorted

educational standards (ej-uh-KAY-shuhn-uhl STAN-durdz) a set of expectations for students, teachers, and schools

formal education (FOR-muhl ej-uh-KAY-shuhn) education that takes place in a school or a structured setting

globalization (GLO-buhl-ih-ZAY-shuhn) the interconnectivity of countries all around the world

literacy rate (LIT-ur-uh-see RAYT) the measurement of a population's ability to read and write

magnet school (MAG-nit SKOOL) a school within a public school system that has a special focus such as math and science or language and the arts

proficiency (pruh-FISH-uhn-see) the ability to do something properly and skillfully

standardized test (STAN-durd-ized TEST) a test given to determine a student's overall competency in one or more subjects

summit (SUHM-it) a meeting of important leaders from different countries

Taliban (TAL-ih-ban) a fundamentalist Muslim group that ruled Afghanistan from 1995 to 2001

taxes (TAKS-ehz) money collected by the government from private citizens that is then used to pay for government programs

tracking (TRAK-eeng) a system in which students are separated into different classes or schools based on their test scores or abilities

For More Information

Books

Doudna, Kelly. *School around the World.*
Edina, MN: Abdo Publishing, 2004.

Lewis, Suzanne Grant. *Education in Africa.*
Philadelphia, PA: Mason Crest Publishers, 2007.

Web Sites

PBS Africa – My World
pbskids.org/africa/myworld/index.html
Read about how real students in Africa describe their daily lives and schools

U.S. Department of Education
www.ed.gov
Read about how No Child Left Behind works, and how the
American school system functions every day

You Think!
youthink.worldbank.org/issues/education
Learn about issues that schools face all over the world and what you can do to help

INDEX

ABOUT THE AUTHOR

Jason Loeb is passionate about children's education. He is a graduate student in the English and education programs at DePaul University in Chicago. This is his first book.